How to...

MEET ALIENS

By CLIVE GIFFORD

Illustrated by
Scoular Anderson

OXFORD
UNIVERSITY PRESS

For Capella and Lyra – C.G.

OXFORD
UNIVERSITY PRESS

Great Clarendon Street, Oxford OX2 6DP

Oxford University Press is a department of the University of Oxford.
It furthers the University's objective of excellence in research, scholarship,
and education by publishing worldwide in

Oxford New York

Athens Auckland Bangkok Bogotá Buenos Aires Calcutta
Cape Town Chennai Dar es Salaam Delhi Florence Hong Kong Istanbul
Karachi Kuala Lumpur Madrid Melbourne Mexico City Mumbai
Nairobi Paris São Paulo Singapore Taipei Tokyo Toronto Warsaw

with associated companies in Berlin Ibadan

Oxford is a registered trade mark of Oxford University Press
in the UK and in certain other countries

Series devised by Hazel Richardson

Text copyright © Clive Gifford 2001

Illustrations copyright © Scoular Anderson 2001

The moral rights of the author and the artist have been asserted

First published 2001

British Library Cataloguing in Publication Data available

ISBN 0–19–910782–3

1 3 5 7 9 10 8 6 4 2

Printed in the United Kingdom by Cox & Wyman Ltd.

Contents

DO THEY EXIST?

Have you ever looked up at the night sky and wondered, 'are there aliens out there?' It's a big question, possibly the biggest question humans have ever asked. Most scientists think the answer is no, but what if other creatures are wondering the exact same thing on a different planet billions of kilometres away from Earth? It's a mind-blowing possibility.

Well, we know the answer.

For all our fancy technology, space stations and computers, we on Earth don't yet have an answer to the big question. But don't get all disappointed. Not having an answer is not the same as saying that the answer's no. So far, there's been no hard-and-fast proof that extraterrestrial life – that is life on places other than the Earth – exists. But, just as importantly, there's been no proof that it doesn't, either. The Universe is a staggeringly huge place. So far we have only explored the tiniest bit of it. Imagine we are searching the sea for one particular, very special drop of water – so far we've only looked in the nearest rock-pool.

Scientists and astronomers are gradually expanding their search, and as they do, amazing discoveries about the Universe are being made every week. In the past five years, over 40 planets have been discovered orbiting distant stars.

It is highly unlikely that any of these newly-found planets contain life and we are a long way away from being able to investigate them thoroughly. But just imagine if proof eventually emerges of aliens in other star systems. It would be the story of the millennium, especially if we could find some way of making direct contact. Just think what it would be like if we could meet up with them. What would they look like? How would they act? How would we communicate with them? What would they think of us? What could they teach us?

Before you rush off to start hunting for aliens and preparing yourself for that historic meeting, you'll want to read this book. It will tell you all about:

- the debate over whether aliens may have visited Earth in the past

- the most famous UFO sightings and alien abduction cases

- how some people have created UFO and alien hoaxes

- what efforts scientists are making to find aliens

- how a meeting with an alien race might be arranged

CHAPTER ONE

THE VERY IDEA

The idea that aliens might exist isn't new. For hundreds and thousands of years people have wondered about the possibility that we may not be alone.

Aliens alert 1:
Fire, fire!
Egypt, 1500 BC

The earliest recorded sighting of something very strange, possibly alien, was in ancient Egypt around 1500 BC. A 'circle of fire' was reported flying through the sky. Fire also featured heavily in the account of the prophet Ezekiel in the Old Testament of the Bible. He described how he saw, 'a great cloud with brightness around it, and fire flashing forth continually.' He describes living creatures each with four faces and four wings. Could he have seen aliens in their spacecraft?

Let's look for a world with smarter, better-dressed creatures.

Have aliens visited Earth in the past? ....

Many ancient cultures believe that they received visitors from other worlds. The traditions of Australian Aborigines, for example, remember alien spirits called Wandjina and how they used flying crafts to travel to Earth from other worlds. Many cultures boast spookily similar tales and drawings of intelligent visitors from the sky. One of the most famous examples was found at Tassili in the Sahara desert. Carved and painted into the rocks are some astonishing 8000-year-old images of human-like creatures, with what look like astronaut helmets on their heads.

Some extraordinary devices have been unearthed by archaeologists. These seem to show advanced knowledge at work hundreds and thousands of years before modern science made such breakthroughs.

Called 'out-of-place objects', they include an ancient Iraqi electrical cell, made 1600 years before batteries were invented, and some amazingly accurate solar and star calendars put together many centuries ago.

11

Another famous example is the Saqqara Bird, a 2200-year-old model glider found in an ancient Egyptian tomb. It boasts aircraft design that would have impressed aero-engineers of the early 20th century.

Alien airport ....

In the Nazca desert in Peru, there is a collection of lines that form many beautifully constructed drawings of birds and animals. 13,000 straight lines cover a big chunk of the desert – but they were only discovered in 1927 when an aircraft flew over them. This is because the pictures are so huge they can only truly be seen from high in the air. To the eyes of some pro-aliens people, the lines appear to form runways and taxiing areas. Alien airport or fanciful hogwash?

Are you sure this is Heathrow, Simpson?

Are these all just examples of human ingenuity and imagination at work? Probably. Or are they evidence of aliens in the past giving people a helping hand? Unlikely, but some people cling on to such a notion.

Let's move on to recorded history with the first sighting of something strange by a well-known historic figure.

Aliens alert 2: flying shields

Tyre, 322 BC

Alexander the Great was a top-notch military leader and ruler, ruthless but intelligent and a conqueror of much of the known world of his time. In 322 BC, whilst laying seige to the ancient city of Tyre, Alexander saw five 'round silver shields' which circled the city and destroyed its walls with beams of light. Seven years earlier, Big Al had seen a pair of similar shields swooping out of the sky. The most powerful man of his age, who was going to creep up to him and tell him he was bonkers?

Could Alexander the Great simply have seen strange natural phenomena such as odd-shaped clouds or lightning? We know that eclipses, when the Moon blocks out the Sun, were treated with awe, fear and panic. Many ancient cultures feared it meant the end of the world, or at best a visit by gigantic alien creatures, who were blocking out the light. Today, we don't think that an eclipse signals that the Earth's time is up, but we still get pretty excited. Total solar eclipses attract thousands of viewers every year.

Get ready to meet aliens:
MAKE A SOLAR ECLIPSE

WHAT YOU'LL NEED
- ❂ a torch
- ❂ a large orange or grapefruit
- ❂ a golf ball and a table

WHAT TO DO
Place the golf ball about 20 centimetres in front of the grapefruit or orange. Shine a torch directly in line with the two round objects from about 60 centimetres away.

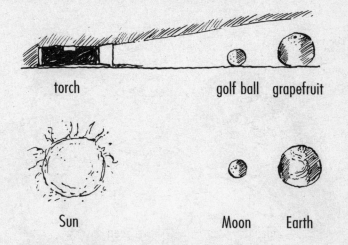

torch   golf ball   grapefruit

Sun   Moon   Earth

WHAT HAPPENS?
You create an eclipse on the fruit's surface. The fruit is the Earth, the golf ball, the Moon and the torch acts like the Sun. The Moon blocks out the Sun's rays and casts a shadow on part of the Earth's surface. The dark centre of the shadow is called the 'umbra'. People within the umbra would see a total eclipse of the Sun.

Earth – the top dog?.............................

The notion of aliens from other worlds didn't really
catch on until more recent times for one important
reason. The Greeks, Romans and many other cultures
believed that Earth was, without doubt, the most
important lump of rock around. It was seen as the
centre of the Universe and the only place where life
existed. The night sky was where the gods or the souls
of the dead hung out according to most religions. In
many lands, anyone who said Earth wasn't top dog
was executed or tortured until they changed their
mind.

It wasn't until the 16th and 17th centuries that people
started to see the real picture. At first, it was kept to a
secret whisper for fear of the authorities stretching you
on the rack, burning you at the stake or lopping your
head off. The Polish astronomer, Copernicus, for
example, kept schtum about his beliefs because he was

afraid of the Church, which was extremely powerful in Europe at the time. But after his death, other astronomers took up his view that the Earth revolved around the Sun and not the other way round. The Sun isn't the centre of the Universe, but it is the centre of our Solar System. And with the arrival of the telescope, more and more was learned about the Universe and Earth's place in it.

Blimey, Galileo, the Moon is incredibly small when viewed through your telescope!

That's because you're looking through the wrong end, my lord.

Dutch spectacle-makers are believed to be the inventors of the telescope in around 1608. Within a year the Italian astronomer, Galileo, improved it enough to make lots of discoveries about the Solar System. There are many different kinds of telescope. This experiment shows you how to build a simple refracting telescope, which uses lenses to magnify then focus the object you are looking at.

17

Get ready to meet aliens:
MAKE A SIMPLE REFRACTING TELESCOPE

WHAT YOU'LL NEED

- ✿ a desk lamp
- ✿ piece of card
- ✿ scissors and sticky tape
- ✿ two magnifying glasses
- ✿ two lumps of modelling clay

WHAT TO DO

Cut a small shape, such as a square or star, out of the centre of the card and tape it onto the front of the desk lamp, making sure it doesn't touch the bulb inside. Shine the lamp onto a dark wall a metre or two away. Push the handle of the magnifying glasses into the lumps of modelling clay to give them a stable base and position one, then both of them in front of the lamp, so that light passes through the lenses of the magnifying glasses.

WHAT HAPPENS?

The light passing through the first magnifying glass forms a blurred circle of light on the wall. This first lens magnifies the image but it is fuzzy and not yet a square or star. Placing the second magnifying glass behind the first brings the image into focus. Adjust the second magnifying glass's position to see how sharp an image you can get.

Small planet – huge Universe ....

As scientists learned more and more about the Universe, Earth's importance shrank and shrank. Our planet, which started off as top dog, fast became an insignificant mongrel pup, lost in the biggest pack of hounds imaginable. Earth turned out to be a relatively small planet, dwarfed by some of the other members of our Solar System, orbiting around a smallish star, the Sun. Our Solar System is a tiny part of an incredibly huge Universe.

How huge? Hope you are ready for some serious numbers. Light travels at a fixed speed, approximately 300,000 kilometres per second. That's pacy. But 300,000 kilometres is too small a unit to describe the enormous distances in space. Astronomers use the light year as a measure of distance. Light travels an awesome 9.5 million million kilometres in a year. One of the nearest star systems to our Solar System is called Alpha Centauri. It's approximately four and a third light years away – that's 41 million million kilometres.

Alpha Centauri is a seriously long distance from Earth, but in the scale of the Universe it's nothing. Our Solar System and Alpha Centauri are part of a galaxy, or collection of stars, called the Milky Way. The nearest galaxy neighbour is about 80,000 light years from Earth and the nearest large galaxy, the Andromeda Galaxy, is more than two million light years away. In anyone's language that is a major league hike, but it is still only a small chunk of the Universe. Scientists speculate as to whether the Universe extends forever and is infinite or is finite and has a definite boundary. Whether it is infinite or finite, astronomers estimate that the farthest we can see in the Universe is between 10 and 15 billion light years. In short, the Universe is unbelievably HUGE!

And how many stars do you reckon inhabit the Universe? Ten thousand? A million? Think again. Astronomers are far from certain, but they reckon that there are AT LEAST 200 billion stars.

Are we the only ones?......................

As Earth's role got smaller and the scale of the Universe got much bigger, some people found it harder to believe that our small planet was the centre of life in the entire Universe. More and more theories started to emerge about life existing in places other than Earth. Mind you, some very smart scientists of their time may have got things a little wrong.

William Herschel was the astronomer who discovered the seventh planet in our Solar System, Uranus. He believed that creatures lived on the Moon and the Sun.

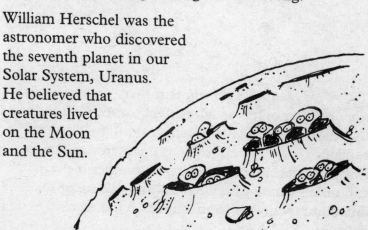

The Swedish chemist, Svante Arrhenius won the 1903 Nobel Prize for chemistry. He believed that life existed everywhere in the Universe and was spread from star to star by tiny seed-like spores.

In 1894 American astronomer Percival Lowell was utterly convinced that the channels he saw on the surface of Mars were canals, part of a massive water-works system built by intelligent Martians.

Today we are pretty certain that there are no canals, nor any kind of life on Mars. We're also fairly clear that most modern tales of aliens and UFOs can be explained away scientifically or uncovered as hoaxes. But potential close encounters with other lifeforms still makes exciting reading. To find out about the different types of close encounters, read on ...

CHAPTER TWO

CLOSE ENCOUNTERS

Unidentified Flying Objects (UFOs) have fascinated people for a long time. People who study these mysterious objects are called ufologists and one of the most famous ufologists is Dr Allan Hynek.

Dr Hyneck invented a simple system for classifying experiences with UFOs, aliens and strange phenomena. It was divided up into long-distance viewings and close encounters – when a witness was within 140 metres of the site. People have added to the system and there are now five classes of close encounter.

Close encounters of:

1   The first kind – when a UFO or strange phenomenon is spotted but it doesn't leave any physical effects.

2   The second kind – when a UFO leaves some sort of measurable effect on the land or on objects around it, such as a scorch mark.

3   The third kind – when moving occupants are spotted, usually inside or next to a UFO.

4   The fourth kind – when human beings are taken from their normal surroundings against their will. This is called abduction.

5   The fifth kind – when humans report direct contact and communication with aliens.

Let's look at some close encounters of the first and second kind, starting with some very strange bright lights in the sky.

Aliens alert 3: Balls and crosses

Europe, 16th-century

On the 7 August 1566 the good people of Basel in Switzerland awoke to find the sky filled with dozens of black globes which became red and fiery before disappearing. Five years earlier, in the German city of Nuremberg, similar black and red balls seemed to fight gigantic red crosses in the sky.

I reckon the crosses will win.

Do you want a bet?

Bright lights ....

Strange glowing features in the sky, like those in Medieval Europe, were reported many times in the 20th century. The astronomer who discovered Pluto, Clyde Tombaugh, saw a bright, hovering light one day but decided not to tell anyone at the time for fear that people would mock his work as a serious astronomer.

American military pilots reported seeing fiery lights that followed their planes. They called the lights foo fighters and thought they were some sort of allied secret weapon. After the war ended, it turned out that German and Japanese pilots had had similar experiences and had thought the same thing. No one has ever explained what all these experienced pilots saw.

Flying saucers.......................................

Bright lights may be strange but they're nothing compared to full-on flying saucer fever. This kicked off in the late 1940s, especially after the experiences of businessman, Kenneth Arnold. He was flying his plane over the Cascade Mountains in Washington on 24 June 1947 when he saw nine crescent-shaped craft flying in formation. He timed them with his watch, and found that they were travelling at a speed of over 2500 kilometres an hour – which was unheard of in aircraft at that time. When he landed, Arnold told all to the press. He described the movement of the craft, 'like a saucer would if you skipped it across the water.' Arnold never used the words flying saucer – but that was the term that found its way onto the front pages of the newspapers.

Want to see for yourself how information can get changed and exaggerated? Try out the following simple activity.

Get ready to meet aliens:
HOW MISINFORMATION CAN OCCUR

WHAT YOU'LL NEED
- ✪ as many friends as you can muster
- ✪ a large open space

WHAT TO DO
Copy out the following message onto a scrap of paper.
'On the 4 April, at 11.30 am, I saw a black UFO 30 metres wide and 13 metres long. It had three small aerials, wings and four bright blue lights.'
Stand your friends in a line twenty paces apart. Tell them that when they receive the message, they have to sprint to the next person in the line and repeat it quickly to them. Don't let anyone in on your original message. After you read out the message to the first person, run to the end of the line to be the very last person to receive the final version.

...three small alien things in bright blue tights.

WHAT HAPPENS?
Don't expect to receive the exact same message you delivered. The numbers and details may have got mixed up and people may have added their own terms in place of yours. This sort of misinformation is more likely to occur when people are excited or distressed, such as after seeing a UFO.

Alien invasion! ....

Within days of Kenneth Arnold's experience, sightings of similar objects started to flood in from all over the world. In the United States alone, 850 people claimed to have seen strange flying saucers in the two months after Arnold's sighting. Some may have been hoaxes or people's imaginations getting the better of them. Yet some sightings by experienced pilots were harder to explain away.

Aliens alert 4:
Buzzed by UFOs

Portugal, 1957

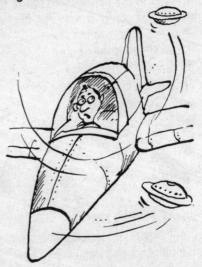

One of the most famous air-to-air encounters with UFOs occurred in September 1957. Four Portuguese airforce F-84 aircraft came across five glowing metallic discs. The discs showed incredible speed and agility, zipping around and in between the aircraft, before shooting vertically upwards and out of sight. One of the pilots, Captain Jose Ferreira insisted that, 'Whatever we saw up there was real, and intelligently controlled. And it scared the hell out of us.'

Close encounters and aliens..................

Close encounters of the third kind, shortened to CE3s, are where aliens are seen as well as UFOs. Most aliens sighted in these reports are similar to humans with just the one over-sized head, two arms and two legs, although their size varies from just over a metre to three-metre giants. The most famous CE3 is the Roswell incident in the United States (see page 53) but another famous example occurred in Shrewsbury, England.

Aliens alert 5: Suits you!

England, 1954

In 1954, Jennie Roestenberg and her children saw a UFO hovering about their house in Shrewsbury. Two creatures could be seen through clear panels on the side of the craft. They had high foreheads, very large eyes and were wearing turquoise suits, a lot like ski suits.

Are you sure the ski slope is near here, Zarg?

Abduction! ....

The scariest of all close encounters, this is where direct contact is made by aliens whether people want it or not. Many of the people who are abducted, called abductees, are somehow transported away to an alien ship where they are investigated or studied in some way.

The first widely reported case of alien abduction occurred in the American state of New Hampshire in 1961. Husband and wife, Betty and Barney Hill, were driving home late one night when they passed close to a UFO. The next thing they remembered at the time was driving away, but two hours had gone missing. Ten days later, Betty began to have severe nightmares in which aliens took them from their car and examined them in a spaceship. Under hypnosis, both Betty and Barney recalled the abduction, could describe their abductors in detail, and their stories matched. But nothing can be proved.

The places where people are abducted from vary widely. Many are abducted from their own beds – which some sceptics think means that they just had a really vivid dream. Yet whether they are taken from a lonely road or their own bedroom, most abductees appear to undergo some common experiences. Abductees often feel unwell after the event, may have marks or scars on them and they frequently suffer from memory loss.

Abductees often disappear for hours which they cannot later account for. In Travis Walton's case, it was six days. The woodcutting crew he was with in 1975 saw a glowing UFO which hit Walton with a beam of light. The crew fled and Walton disappeared for six days. When he reappeared, he claimed he had been abducted and examined, and had eventually escaped. When tested with a lie detector, the readings strongly suggested he was telling the truth.

The fifth kind: communication ....

A small number of people claim that they have
directly communicated with aliens. Radio enthusiast
Richard Miller, for example, claimed he tuned in to
radio messages telling him where to meet with aliens.

Taken aboard their
spaceship, Miller was
shown key events in
mankind's history
including the start of the
Universe – the Big Bang.

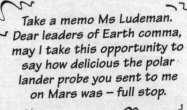

Another famous example
is Marge Ludeman. She
claimed to have received
more than 500 messages
from an alien commander
called Hilarion dictated
to her via thought
waves from outer
space.

Sounds crazy? It may well be, but it is interesting that many contactees claim that the communication was made by telepathy, that is sending or receiving messages without using any of our five senses of sight, hearing, touch, taste or smell. Much research has gone into trying to prove whether telepathy or other forms of extra-sensory perception exist amongst humans gifted with a sixth sense. And you can join in the hunt with your version of a famous ESP experiment, below.

Get ready to meet aliens:
TRY OUT A FAMOUS ESP EXPERIMENT

WHAT YOU'LL NEED
- a piece of card
- a pen
- scissors
- a notebook
- two large hardback books
- a volunteer

WHAT TO DO

Cut the card into five similar-sized pieces and draw one of the five symbols on the previous page — a circle, a square, a set of three wavy lines, a five-pointed star, and a plus sign — on each. Put the two books up on a table to completely shield your cards and notebook and sit your volunteer on the other side. Shuffle the pack and pick a card, but DON'T show it to your friend. Ask your friend to call out what symbol they think you have picked. Avoid giving any hints or signs. Use your notebook to scribble down whether they were right or wrong and then shuffle and pick another card. Do this ten times in all, then total up the score.

That's ten out of ten for the third time — are you an alien?

WHAT HAPPENS?

You are performing a version of what is known as the Rhine Experiment. There's a one in five chance that your friend will call a card correctly. If your friend gets eight or nine right, re-test them. If they get the same high score again, they may have ESP!

Many people maintain that ESP, close encounters, aliens and UFOs can all be explained by science or common sense. Let's have a look at some of the reasons and explanations they give.

CHAPTER THREE

HOAXES, THE WEATHER AND OTHER RATIONAL EXPLANATIONS

A sensible, scientific explanation ....

If you want to be a UFO investigator and possibly meet aliens in the future, then you have to be scientific about it. Scientists, even those who believe in the possibility of aliens, know that many reports are not UFOs at all. OK then, what are they? Here's a list of some of the most common explanations.

- clouds and other atmospheric phenomena
- man-made rockets and satellites orbiting Earth
- planets and stars
- helicopters
- weather balloons
- secret jet planes

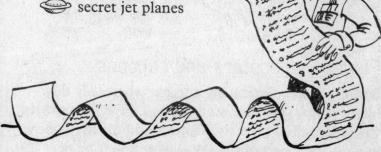

35

It's just the weather ....

There's no question that extraordinary weather patterns or features are responsible for many UFO sightings. There's a type of cloud called lenticular cloud, which forms when winds blow over mountain tops. Lenticular clouds can form outrageously convincing saucer shapes. Some fiery spheres in the sky can be put down to a really weird sort of lightning called ball lightning. Scientists don't fully understand how it forms or travels, but these football or smaller-sized globes of lightning occur after a thunderstorm and do drift through the air – giving the impression of being under control.

No, Geoff, that's not the ...

Planes, helicopters and balloons............

Some aircraft, particularly at night when only their lights can be seen, are reported as UFOs. The stories where the UFO's lights disappear and then re-appear in a different part of the sky can, at times, be put down to the aircraft flying through clouds. Helicopters at night have also been known to confuse people because of their ability to hover and move in any direction. Other important man-made objects that can get mistaken for alien technology are airships and weather balloons that are sent into the Earth's atmosphere to record temperatures and air pressures. Many of these are made of shiny, silver-coloured material designed to reflect sunlight. From certain angles, the material can look like metal.

The night sky

After the Moon, the brightest object in the night sky is Venus. Lots of eyewitnesses who report viewing a strange glowing light have, in fact, been watching a planet over 40 million kilometres away. Many rockets heading upwards on their launch have been mistaken for fast moving alien craft. And so have satellites in low orbits around Earth, and small pieces of asteroid rock and dust, known as meteors, heading towards Earth.

Now, here's an amazing fact. There are as many as 22,000 pieces of space junk orbiting the Earth. Broken satellites, discarded parts of rockets, debris from explosions, all make up a belt of human-made objects travelling in orbit around Earth. Some of these pieces re-enter the Earth's atmosphere.

Hoax!..

A hoax is when someone lies or deliberately misleads people about what they have seen. Hoaxers have sometimes gone as far as creating phoney photos, marks in the ground, and fake aliens and UFOs. Hoaxes have sometimes been very successful with many people believing them until they are disproven. People even fall for tall tales of aliens or other strange phenomena even when they're just fiction. In 1938, a radio play version of the sci-fi book *War of the Worlds* caused panic in the United States. Given the full spooky treatment by a young actor, Orson Welles, people genuinely believed that Martians had invaded and were running riot – even though it wasn't intended to mislead!

Aliens alert 6:
Look who's talking!
USA, 1969

In October 1969 an American called Jimmy Carter witnessed a UFO. He told reporters, 'It was the darndest thing I've ever seen. It was big. It was very bright, it changed colours ... We watched it for ten minutes, but none of us could figure out what it was.' Was Carter just another trickster trying to pull a hoax on the authorities? No, not at all. He was a respected former naval engineer and farmer, who in 1976 became president of the United States!

Some hoaxes are just plain silly and pretty simple to prove wrong. In the January 1978 issue of American magazine, *Official UFO*, an article claimed that, five months earlier, the town of Chester, Illinois had been wiped out by hostile UFOs.

The people of that town protested. They were still around, felt fine and hadn't seen one UFO let alone an attacking fleet. The owner of the magazine didn't flinch from his story. He claimed that the aliens in the UFO attack fleet rebuilt the town in an instant!

Others are more believable and can trick people for years. Whether silly or clever, hoaxes further undermine claims that aliens have visited Earth, claims that many people do not take seriously in the first place.

Why hoax? ....

Why would someone bother to go to all these lengths?
Is the pursuit of fame and fortune reason enough?
Most hoaxes haven't been anonymous photos or
evidence sent in to a government or the media. Nearly
all hoaxers go public, and in doing so they often get
their story and photos published, or even write a
bestselling book about their experiences.

Some hoaxers do it just for a laugh. One of the most
successful photo hoaxes was performed by a pair of
schoolkids from Sheffield, England, back in 1962.
They produced a photo of a formation of five flying
saucers swooping over their home town. Newspapers
rushed to print calling it, 'the best UFO photograph
ever'. The best hoax photograph, perhaps. Ten years
later, one of the boys admitted that they had faked the
picture by painting five saucer shapes on a piece of
glass and then taking a photograph through it.

41

Bet you fancy trying your hand at a bit of hoaxing trickery? Don't worry, this chapter has three ingenious projects to cook up your own aliens and UFO piccies. Here's the first.

Want something to appear enormous or very small? Just as hoaxers before you, you can use simple trick photography to merge a close-up and a distant image into one picture.

Get ready to meet aliens:
FAKE THAT PHOTO

WHAT YOU'LL NEED
- ✪ a camera
- ✪ a film
- ✪ several friends
- ✪ a long stretch of flat land (a beach would be ideal)

WHAT TO DO
Stand a few metres away from friend A. Ask the others to walk back 40–50 paces, keeping in a straight line.
Then ask friend A to stick out their hand, palm upwards. Move your camera so that your friends in the distance appear to be standing on friend A's hand. Take a few pictures.

WHAT HAPPENS?
When you get your pictures back, you should have some stunning images of small creatures standing on your friend's hand. If you like what you see, try it again but get your friends to dress up to look less like humans and more like aliens.

If you haven't got a camera to hand but have some snaps from your last holiday, you can still create a hoax picture by trying out this easy project.

Nowadays, with personal computers able to alter pictures on screen, it is even easier to make impressive fake photos.

For photos to be taken seriously, they now have to be backed up by sightings and accounts from a number of independent witnesses. Still, it shouldn't stop you from having a little fun – turning a friend or someone in your family into an extraterrestrial.

Get ready to meet aliens:
TURN YOUR MUM (OR DAD OR LITTLE SISTER) INTO AN ALIEN

WHAT YOU'LL NEED
- ✪ a photo of your family member on as light a background as possible
- ✪ access to a computer scanner and a personal computer which has image editing software (Windows 98 and 2000 machines have a simple image editor built in)

WHAT TO DO
Pop the photo under the scanner and scan it into the computer. You now have a computer version of the photo as a file. If you've not used graphics or image editing programs before, get a friend who has to help you. Try stretching the face and body of your subject, enlarging their eyes or adding extra facial features.

➤

Oh, honestly, Howard..........................

Some people fake whole alien encounters, not just
photos. Howard Menger announced in 1956 that he
was in contact with friendly aliens from Venus. He
claimed that he helped disguise them on Earth, and in
past lives had even travelled to Saturn. Even at the
time much of Menger's story and his photos looked
phoney. Since then, space probes to Venus and Saturn
have proven that life as Menger described it could not
exist on those planets.

Thanks for the disguise,
Howard. Now, I will definitely fit in
here on Earth.

Aliens alert 7:
By George, it's a fake, isn't it?
USA, 1940s

George Adamski's case is one of the most famous and controversial. He claimed to have been befriended by aliens who used telepathy to warn him of the damage to the Solar System created by testing nuclear weapons. Adamski claimed that the aliens gave him a tour of their ship, allowed him to take photos of the outside and, later, took him on trips to Venus and Mars. Amazingly, lots of people believed him, even though his photos were reckoned to be fakes. He liked to be called 'professor' and made people think he worked at the Palomar Observatory as a big-brained boffin. In fact, George Adamski worked in a hot-dog restaurant at the foot of Palomar Mountain! The debate still continues — alien communicator or fast-food fraudster?

We need a better home world for our alien craft than Planet Ketchup, Bob.

Project Blue Book.................................

Although cases like Menger's and Adamski's look phoney, the US government was worried enough about other cases of UFOs and aliens to make a list of reports and investigate them. Project Blue Book, as it became known, has been surrounded in myth – but here are the key, 100 per cent accurate facts.

- It started in 1948 and was closed down in 1969.

- It investigated over 12,000 reports and logically explained most away as mistaken aircraft, weather or star sightings.

- It was criticized by many ufologists for being anti aliens and UFOs from the start.

- It decided that UFOs were not a threat to national or world security.

- But it was unable to explain 701 reports.

Around the world, almost 13 million people have seen phenomena they believe to be aliens or UFOs. Around half a million cases may fall into the same unexplained category as Project Blue Book's 701 mysteries. What if governments do know the answers to the remaining puzzlers? What if they are already in league with aliens, or have built their own flying saucers? Could that be possible? Read on.

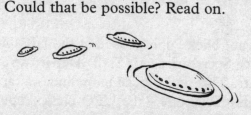

CHAPTER FOUR

CONSPIRACIES

Do you ever think that someone's keeping something from you? Of course you do. Many people don't think it's just their little sister or best mate not telling them where their sweets are hidden. Some actually think that the governments of some countries know all about aliens and are keeping seriously schtum. And we're not talking about a handful of cranks, either. A 1999 *Newsweek* magazine poll found that 49 per cent of Americans thought the government were hiding information on UFOs from the people.

Shh.

Civil servant Nick Pope worked at the UK's Ministry of Defence Secretariat (Air Staff) Department 2A for three years. This dull official name hides a far more exciting unofficial title – the UFO Desk. Pope was a real-life Fox Mulder from *The X-Files*, checking out strange events and happenings. He started out an unbeliever, but now is convinced that UFOs are out there. He is also convinced that many military people are afraid of going public for fear of being ridiculed.

But I DID see a UFO, Sarge!

QUIET, Jackson. You've got another 300 push-ups to go.

Aliens alert 8: Fire in the forest
England, 1980

One famous example of a military hush-up occurred in December 1980. Two military men from RAF Woodbridge reported a dazzling fire in nearby Rendlesham Forest and spotted a strange triangular object, which shot off faster than any aircraft the two men had ever seen. The deputy base commander, Lieutenant Colonel Charles Halt, saw the same thing the next night. Halt's photographs and report were confiscated by the US military and never released.

Is it a bird, is it a plane …?

Could the sighting in Rendlesham Forest have been a top-secret project built on Earth? One of the strongest conspiracy theories is that many UFOs are actually incredibly advanced military craft being tested out in hush-hush conditions. We now know about amazing planes like the superfast SR71 *Blackbird* and the Stealth bomber, the B2. But in the past, when they were being tested, it is likely that tests on them accounted for some UFO sightings.

Aliens alert 9: Throwing shapes
UK and Belgium, 1989–90

Between December 1989 and 1990, more than 13,500 reports of a bizarre wedge-shaped UFO poured in from the UK and Belgium. The eyewitnesses included radar operators, police officers and air-force pilots. On nine different occasions, jet fighters were scrambled to intercept the black craft, more than 60 metres wide, but every time the craft was able to zip away undetected.

If you're tired of orbs, cigars and saucer shapes, check out our new Buzz 7 triangular craft.

Could these sightings have been test flights of a top-secret, triangular-wing aircraft called *Waverider* or *Loflyte*? It's rumoured that such a high-speed plane may have been built by NASA and the US air force. If so, why didn't the authorities own up to a prototype and save a lot of fuss and bother?

Area 51

About 130 kilometres north-west of the American city of Las Vegas, lie 20,200 square kilometres of military land totally off-limits to the public. Called the Groom Lake Air Force Base, even airliners are not allowed to fly directly above it. Within this base lies a section known as Dreamland, or Area 51. This is the most notorious military area around.

It's believed that many American aircraft projects, particularly spy and stealth planes, have been developed and tested there – and still are. For years, the United States government and military wouldn't admit that such a place existed, despite the claims of people who once worked there. But Russian satellite pictures posted on the Internet in 2000 revealed that the base is there and that it boasts the world's longest runway – 9.7 kilometres of it. The photos also show underground buildings, strange crater shapes dotted around the compound – and even tennis courts.

Could Area 51 be the location for things more amazing than the latest spy planes? Many people believe that fragments of recovered aliens or their craft are held at this top-secret base. Perhaps, deep in its stores, lies the truth about the most famous conspiracy theory of the lot – crashed aliens at Roswell, New Mexico.

The Roswell Incident ....

It all started with a string of UFO sightings in late June 1947. Farmer Mac Brazel came across some silvery wreckage made of a strange material. The airforce base near the town was eventually contacted, and an intelligence officer called Major Jesse Marcel investigated the scene. Brazel was taken in for questioning and emerged almost a week later to change his story and agree with the official line that it was a new type of weather balloon. Brazel never spoke about the incident again, even to members of his own family.

Around the same time, a civil engineer called Grady Burnett found a disc-shaped object crashed in a field. He claimed that nearby were the bodies of four hairless creatures, 1.5 metres tall, with large pear-shaped heads and thin arms and legs. They had no ears and were wearing one-piece suits. The crash site was quickly sealed-off by military personnel. The official story, once again, was that it was a balloon.

This story was pretty much accepted until the 1970s, when Major Marcel admitted that he had been part of a cover-up operation. Detailed witness reports were gathered by ufologists. Sadly, Grady Barnett had already died, but others recalled alien bodies being recovered and even medical examinations being performed upon them at the airbase hospital. Recently, the US military has changed its story. They have admitted that the cover-up was to protect a new sort of spying balloon, and that the 'aliens' were in fact crash test dummies thrown from research balloons. Story over? Not quite. Why are the authorities now admitting to any human-like objects being found at the crash site? And why weren't the dummies more human-like? No one is telling … well, not yet anyway.

In 1995, sensational footage of an autopsy being performed on one of the Roswell aliens was shown. It was probably a hoax, but it has brought the strange events at Roswell and the possible cover-up there back into the limelight.

The Greys

The creatures at Roswell may or may not have been Greys – the most commonly described type of alien.

A TYPICAL 'GREY'

1–1.5 m tall.
Very slender.

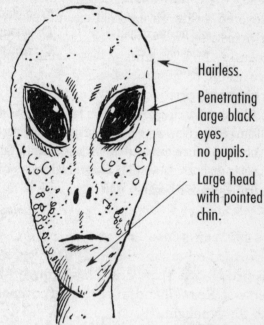

Hairless.

Penetrating large black eyes, no pupils.

Large head with pointed chin.

Conspiracy theorists believe that the Greys crashed one or more of their spaceships, and that this was found by the US government. The government negotiated a secret treaty with the aliens and allowed them to take a small number of human samples (abductees) for temporary observation. In return, the aliens let the government into the secrets of some of their technology. There are two endings to this story – either the Greys didn't keep up their side of the bargain, or they did release some details, which could be being worked on within Area 51.

Get ready to meet aliens:
MAKE A HEAD OF A GREY

WHAT YOU'LL NEED
- a large round balloon
- lots of newspaper
- wallpaper paste
- a bowl
- a plastic or paper cup
- water-based paints
- a paintbrush

WHAT TO DO
Mix up the wallpaper paste in a bowl and tear the newspaper into pieces. Blow up the balloon and tie the neck with a piece of string before resting it in the paper cup. Build up layers of paper and glue around the balloon, taking care to cover the top half of the paper cup as well.

Leave to set. Once hard, cut the bottom off the cup. Reach inside and untie the string to let the air out of the balloon and remove the balloon. Gently dent two palm-sized areas on the balloon for the eye areas, and first paint the whole head a shade of grey before filling in the details of the Grey's large black eyes, slit-like nose and mouth.

➤

From Greys to Men in Black...............

If events like Roswell and the sightings of Greys really occurred, wouldn't we know about them? Not necessarily, argue some people. Not if governments work really hard to keep it all quiet. The 1998 film of the same name painted the Men in Black as friendly heroes, saving Earth from hostile aliens. Many people reckon they've encountered real-life Men in Black, and they're nowhere near as friendly. They threaten people who claim to have experienced close encounters to keep silent or else.

Men in Black, or MIBs for short, wear black suits, sunglasses and drive around in unmarked large black cars. Although the cars look brand new, they always

57

appear to be an old design. The same thing is true of their dress and sunglasses. Are they shady government agents or could they be aliens in a time warp?

But when we received images of this planet 30 of their years ago, that was what they were wearing!

The first documented occurrence of MIB happened in 1953. Albert K. Bender was the editor of a flying-saucer magazine called *Space Review*. In the October issue, Bender put in an announcement saying that he had uncovered information that would solve the flying-saucer mystery, but had been ordered not to print it. The magazine closed down soon after. In a later interview, Bender admitted he had been visited by three Men in Black and had been 'scared to death' of them.

You want holiday shorts and Hawaiian shirt in BLACK, Sir?

Another case of MIB happened in December 1979, shortly after the alleged abduction of Frenchman, Franck Fontaine. One of the witnesses, Jean-Pierre Prevost, was called upon by three MIB. They warned him not to say a word about his experiences. Prevost maintained that their eyes were pure white and they were terrifying. Other UFO and alien eyewitnesses claim to have had similar experiences, but no government will admit to their existence.

Astronauts and aliens ....

Who would you trust most to spot an alien: your maths teacher, a politician or an astronaut? Surely, astronauts are well-equipped to recognize satellites and stars so that when they report something strange, they're less likely to be mistaken. In June 1965, astronauts Ed White (the first American to walk in space) and James McDivitt were passing over Hawaii in a Gemini spacecraft when they saw a weird-looking metallic object. The UFO had long arms sticking out of it. McDivitt took pictures with a cine-camera. Those pictures have never been released.

The conspiracy theory goes that NASA knows all about lots of UFO sightings by astronauts in space, but has kept them under wraps. One of the most staggering claims concerns the 1969 *Apollo 11* Moon landing. It is alleged that Neil Armstrong – the first man to set foot on the Moon – saw two UFOs in a nearby crater. He blabbed about them in surprise at the time but NASA censored the news in the transmission made to the public. Ten years after the event, Maurice Chatelain, former chief of NASA communications systems, claimed, 'The encounter was common knowledge in NASA, but nobody has talked about it until now.'

Fantasy or conspiracy, the search for the truth about aliens continues. Check out the next chapter to see what scientists and ufologists are doing to detect intelligent alien life.

CHAPTER FIVE

THE SEARCH FOR ALIEN LIFE

Hunt the alien ....

There are two ways to hunt for aliens. The first is to investigate the strange events happening on Earth. The second is to look away from Earth, to distant stars and galaxies which may contain extraterrestrial life.

Don't interrupt me. Can't you see I'm searching the Universe for alien life?

Away from Earth ....

The search away from Earth really started with the
invention of space probes and new types of telescope.
Space probes are unmanned machines carrying
measuring equipment, which are sent to land on or fly
past other planets. The sights these space probes have
shown us have excited space scientists, but
disappointed those holding out for life in our Solar
System. The probes have measured things like what
the planet's surface and atmosphere are made of.
What they have found appears to prove that life as we
know it could not exist there.

Scientists will continue to explore our Solar System because there is still so much to learn about it. For example, recent data about one of Jupiter's moons, Europa, points to the small chance that oceans of water could lie beneath its cracked, icy surface. It would be foolish not to check such fascinating possibilities out.

But the serious search for aliens is happening far away from our Solar System. The Universe is so huge, and contains so many millions of star systems, that you'd think it's likely there are systems and planets which could support life out there somewhere.

Tuning in ....

We cannot send space probes to the far reaches of the Universe, yet, but we can send and receive radio signals over huge distances. Radio telescopes are being used to scour the Universe for signs or signals of alien intelligence. In 1960 astronomer Frank Drake started Project Ozma, which became known as the Search for Extraterrestrial Intelligence (SETI).

SETI is a long-term, ongoing mission. It mainly monitors some of the radio waves, which don't carry sound, that come from different parts of the Universe, looking for sequences of radio signals which don't appear random. It's a huge task – as the following experiment shows.

Get ready to meet aliens:
SEE WHAT SETI IS UP AGAINST

WHAT YOU'LL NEED
- a spare room
- as many radios, tape recorders, CD players and televisions as possible

WHAT TO DO
Ask permission to borrow your family's audio equipment and put it all into a room with plenty of electrical plug sockets. Switch all the different machines on, tune them into talk rather than music programmes and adjust the volumes to around the same level. Stand in the middle of the room and pick one radio to try to concentrate on for a minute or so.

And the winning lottery numbers are...

Net gains

SETI is involved in a number of projects, one of which is roping in thousands of Internet users to help with their work. Called SETI@Home, it involves downloading a special screensaver. The screensaver program uses your machine when you are not, to work through some of the radio wave-data their telescope receives, searching for patterns amongst the random noise – patterns which could indicate the presence of intelligent life.

Who knows, in a year or two from now, your computer may just be the one which discovers some sign of alien life trying to make contact!

Aliens alert 10: Radio daze

USA, 1977

On 15 August 1977, SETI equipment at the Ohio State Radio Observatory in the United States picked up a really powerful and distinct radio signal. When astronomer Dr Jerry Ehman saw the signal's printout from the telescope, he was amazed and couldn't help writing 'WOW!' next to it. As hard as people tried, the signal wasn't detected again. There's a possibility that it genuinely came from deep space.

Check this, it sounds like an alien broadcast.

Bob, you've been away from chart music too long, it's just Techno.

Fingers on the pulsar

So far, SETI hasn't found anything definitely alien in the airwaves. Radio astronomy in general, however, has lead to important discoveries about the Universe, such as finding pulsars. In 1967, astronomer Jocelyn

Bell was using a radio telescope when she picked up a regular pulsing radio signal every 1.3 seconds. This was no random background noise from the Universe. Bell even wrote LGM (short for Little Green Men) next to the printout of the signals. What Bell had discovered wasn't an alien intelligence but a new type of object in the skies, a dying star called a pulsar. Astronomers have since learned that pulsars are the cores of large stars which have collapsed in on themselves. They send out narrow beams of radio waves as they spin.

Get ready to meet aliens:
MAKE YOUR OWN PULSAR

WHAT YOU'LL NEED
- ✪ a torch
- ✪ a long piece of string
- ✪ something to hang the string securely from

➤

Where to search? ....

Good question. With the search for extraterrestrial life rather like looking for a needle in a million haystacks, any handy hints on which haystacks to look in would be welcomed. Powerful radio and optical telescopes are increasing our knowledge of the Universe constantly. They are also beginning to discover far more planets orbiting sun-like stars than we previously thought existed. In the past seven years or so, more than 40 planets have been found. Many of these planets are unlikely to be suitable for supporting life. Yet one day we may hit upon a planet that is.

Some people claim there may be clues about where to look right here on Earth, for instance the experiences of the Dogon tribe.

Aliens alert 11:
Well, I'll be Dogon

Mali, before 3000 BC

The Dogon people of Mali, West Africa, have had a staggering knowledge of astronomy for thousands of years. Long before the telescope was invented, the Dogon knew about rings around Saturn, they knew that we were part of a spiral galaxy (the Milky Way) and that the Earth revolves around the Sun. According to Dogon tradition, they were taught all this by an alien race called the Nommos, who come from a planet that orbits a third Sirius star just under nine light years away from Earth.

Astronomers originally scoffed. There wasn't even a second small and heavy Sirius star as the Dogon's predicted, let alone a third.

The Dogon's claims are absolute...

Hang on...

Gulp!

Sirius B was photographed for the first time in 1970. Astronomers believe it is actually a small, heavy type of star called a white dwarf. So far, the third Sirius star has not been located — are the Dogons having us on, or is modern science still trying to catch up?

Hi, Earth here...

Searching for aliens is vital work, but there is another side – giving aliens every chance of finding us. Our searching technology may be too limited at the moment. We should also try to make ourselves as noticeable as possible in case extraterrestrials are searching too.

One of the first suggestions for signalling aliens came from German mathematician, Karl Friedrich Gauss. In 1815, he suggested planting trees in huge formations. Now that people have orbited Earth, we know that even the biggest forest wouldn't attract attention from space.

Instead, several space probes have journeyed out of the Solar System carrying details about the human race and the planet we live on. Radio telescopes, normally used to receive signals, have occasionally sent signals into deep space as well. In 1974, the Arecibo radio telescope sent a coded message. It was made up of radio pulses which detailed Earth's position in the Solar System, a simple image of a human being and the way in which the message was sent. It's hoped that the signal may one day be picked up and understood by a distant alien civilization. Don't wait up – it could take a very, very long time.

Right, folks. This dish-like creature sent the message from the Milky Way.

Searching Earth

Back on Earth, ufologists are still busy examining reports and testimony from past and current close encounters. Ufologists have to be good at many things. Ufologists have to wear many hats.

They need to be expert interviewers as they document witnesses' accounts. They must be good campaigners to get files released from government archives. They must also be as scientific as possible when they visit landing or incident sites. This means collecting evidence carefully and not jumping to conclusions.

It can also mean using photography and other methods to measure and record all the details.

UFO hotspots on Earth........................

Ufologists tend to concentrate their research on areas with lots of reports of alien and UFO activity. These are known as hotspots and you'll want to know where some of these can be found.

New Mexico, USA:
home of Area 51, not far from Roswell and a regular haven for UFOs.

East coast of USA:
hundreds of encounters are reported in this part of the United States every year.

Belgium:
this small country's most famous wave of sightings were of triangular craft (see page 50).

Japan:
the north island of Japan, Hokkaido, is a common source of UFO reports.

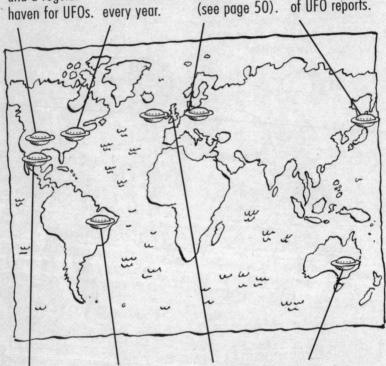

Mexico:
the capital, Mexico City, has been regularly buzzed by UFOs, according to eyewitnesses.

Brazil:
has one of the highest UFO sighting rates in the world.

Great Britain:
a top place for UFO spotting, especially the south and south-west of England and Scotland.

Australia:
the area around the cities of Adelaide and Melbourne is considered a major hotspot by ufologists.

There are many other places around the world where UFOs have been spotted and people claim to have been abducted.

Just before you jet off to investigate, have you packed your UFO detector kit, and have you tested it out on a pretend landing site? You mean, you haven't? Well, you had better put one together and road test it, as the following activity explains.

Get ready to meet aliens:
BUILD AND USE A DETECTOR KIT

WHAT YOU'LL NEED
As many of the following items as you can get together:
- a pencil
- a thermometer
- a magnifying glass
- some sealable plastic freezer bags
- a ruler and/or a tape measure
- a compass
- an eye dropper and small bottle of water
- a notebook
- gloves
- tweezers

WHAT TO DO
Find a spot in your garden or in some open land and pretend it's the site of a close encounter. Before you approach the site, use the compass to establish North and the thermometer to measure the regular air temperature.
Study the site hard and note down the air temperature, weather and any other details in your notebook. Use the compass again to see if any strange magnetic readings alter the way the compass points. If you find any depressions in the ground or strange markings on trees or rocks, sketch and measure them.

➤

Any small objects of interest should be picked up with tweezers, examined with a magnifying glass and then put in a freezer bag as an exhibit. Larger items should be tested for heat by placing the thermometer close to them and checking for any great change in temperature, before you pick them up with gloves and place them in a bag.

Boy, that's hot!

WHAT HAPPENS?

Well, unless you have amazingly stumbled on a landing site, very little, but the skills you learn in taking down local details will stand you in good stead if you ever find a hotspot of your own. A full-on UFO detector kit would also include a camera and film, binoculars (never pointed anywhere near the Sun) and materials to make plaster casts.

Whether you're looking far out into space, or close to Earth, you'll want to know just what you may be looking for. The next chapter is all about alien biology and how this could affect meeting and communicating with creatures from other worlds.

CHAPTER SIX

ALIEN BIOLOGY

The usual suspects ....

Let's first look at some of the most common sorts of
aliens reported by those experiencing close
encounters.

Notice anything about the line-up? Those who don't
believe in aliens have. They wonder how come all the
most popular aliens are humanoid (human-like) in
appearance, with four limbs, two eyes and one head.

One answer may be that if aliens really have the technology to visit Earth as we speak, then perhaps they also have the ability to dress up or change shape to mimic the planet's inhabitants.

Okay, so which of these Earth things is the intelligent one?

DRESSING UP BOX

And it's important to remember that some close encounters have been with creatures which were definitely not human-like in appearance.

Aliens alert 12: Lizard Kings?
USA, 1983

One day farmers Ron and Paula Watson saw a lizard-like creature on a neighbouring farm in the American state of Missouri. Its skin was green and scaly. Here's the really scary part. The couple estimated it to be 2 metres in height! ➤

Most scientists reckon we shouldn't expect aliens' real forms to be human-like for serious scientific reasons. We're going to look at two of the most important – evolution on Earth and the conditions found on other planets.

Evolution

We have learned that life on our planet has evolved over millions and millions of years. To get to human beings, evolution has been through billions of stages and changes. The chances of it going through the exact same processes on another planet to produce the same or similar results are incredibly slim. Even if a planet had a similar set-up, it would be very likely to produce quite different creatures.

This creature, called Arnold, was designed by a biologist to show how life could have evolved on Earth if different creatures had survived.

And even if Earth's exact twin planet was somewhere out there in the Universe, what are the chances of catching it at the same stage of evolution as our planet? Humans consider themselves the highest form of life on Earth, but millions of years ago we didn't exist. Evolution is a continuing process – who knows what will be the planet's most dominant or intelligent creature in the distant future?

80

No comparison......................................

One major problem in discussing alien biology is that we don't have anything other than Earth's collection of creatures to compare it with. In chemistry, when scientists were discovering new elements they had dozens to act as a guide. When biologists found new plants or animals they, too, had plenty of others to act as a reference. When thinking about life on another, possibly quite different, planet from our own, all we have as a guide is Earth.

So how can we consider what aliens could look like? Well, one way is to take key features of a planet like its atmosphere, temperature and gravity, and think how these could affect life on other worlds.

Atmosphere......................................

The atmosphere is the blanket of gases around a planet. Astronomers believe that the atmospheres of the other planets in our Solar System aren't suitable to sustain life. Atmospheres around planets in other parts of the Milky Way, or in other galaxies, may have more suitable atmospheres for life. The pressure of the atmosphere, its thickness and what it is made up of would have a huge effect on the types of creatures that could live there.

To get enough important gases from its planet's atmosphere, this creature has its 'lungs' outside its main body – and boy, are they massive!

Temperature ....

The atmosphere around a planet and the strength of the heat from the sun it orbits are important factors in creating life. Just as important is the planet's distance from its sun. Astronomers talk about a 'habitable zone' a certain distance away from the Sun, where temperatures aren't too extreme so that liquid water could exist and give a boost to the remote chance of life existing there. To see how distance away from a source of heat can affect temperature, check out the following simple experiment.

Get ready to meet aliens:
MEASURE THE HEAT OF LIGHT

WHAT YOU'LL NEED
- ✪ an adjustable desk lamp
- ✪ two thermometers

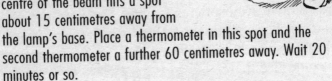

WHAT TO DO
Place the desk lamp on a large table and switch it on. Angle the lamp, as in the picture, so that the centre of the beam hits a spot about 15 centimetres away from the lamp's base. Place a thermometer in this spot and the second thermometer a further 60 centimetres away. Wait 20 minutes or so.

WHAT HAPPENS?
The temperature of the thermometer closest to the light will be a lot higher than the temperature of the thermometer positioned further away. In the same way, planets orbiting a sun will be hotter the closer they are to their sun.

A matter of some gravity ....

Another important factor in alien biology is gravity. Gravity is a force of attraction between objects. It's the pulling force that causes us and everything else to stay put on Earth. But gravitational pull varies depending on where you are in the Universe. On Jupiter, it's more than twice as strong as here, on Mars, only a third as strong. It is possible for life to occur on planets with both a lot less and a lot more gravity than we have on Earth. Lots more gravity might mean that creatures are very small or extremely flat, perhaps with armour to protect themselves from the great pressures on them.

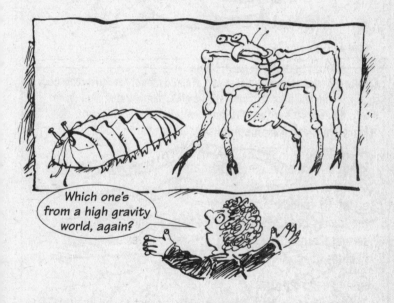

Which one's from a high gravity world, again?

Alien zoo ....

Want to see some more examples of how planetary conditions could affect what alien life looks like? Well, check out the exhibits at our newly opened alien zoo.

Creature A lives on a planet without a solid surface but with an atmosphere which can support life. Its balloon-like body is filled with gas to let it float through the atmosphere and its massive mouth has a filter to let in tiny organisms — its food.

Creature B lives on a dark planet with a dense atmosphere that rains acid, so it has a horned back to protect it. The dark, dense atmosphere means there's no need for eyes and the three tentacle-like tails emit sonar signals to help the creature find its way. A feeding grill runs the length of its body.

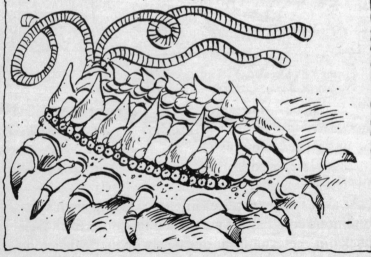

Creature C comes from a planet which lies for most of the time on the edge of the habitable zone but for a short time orbits really close to its sun. It buries itself deep in the ground to insulate it and provide some warmth when away from the sun, massive flaps of skin extend up and outwards to soak in as much heat as possible.

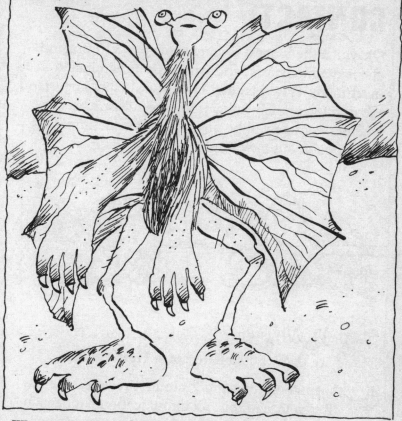

We can see just how remote the chances of us encountering alien life are. But just imagine how all the unbelievers would feel if an extraterrestrial intelligence proved its existence to us. And how would you feel if you were singled out to be the person to make that first scientifically proven contact with aliens from another world? Want to see how it could possibly happen? Turn that page!

CHAPTER SEVEN

CONTACT!

Okay, it's the longest of long shots but let's pretend aliens definitely exist and you've been nominated to meet them. How exciting! How scary! How important! We don't genuinely know if intelligent life exists or whether contact will be possible in our lifetimes, but let's think about how it might possibly happen.

Step 1: Why you?.................................

There are many possible reasons. Here are three:

1   Alien communications are first received the day after you read this. Communication happens in secret for many years before contact is verified. By 2030, you could be a top UFO researcher, a world leader in alien communication. You could be the natural choice for the job.

2   That close encounter you had in 2005 left as big an impression on the aliens as on you. In later communications, they insist on you to make the first public contact.

3   You were the first person to pick up the vital broadcast or telepathic information from the aliens. It may have been while you were working for SETI back on Earth, or while you were working in space or on Mars as one of the first colonists. However it came about, you have been given the honour of making the first symbolic contact.

Step 2: What to say and do? ....

While you are being prepared for your historic mission, there would be the most amazing level of discussion and argument. At the very highest levels, scientists and leaders would be working out every tiny detail of communication, making sure that nothing could be wrongly interpreted. The debate on what to say and what not to say would be incredibly intense. So much would be at stake.

Get ready to meet aliens:
BE A WORLD LEADER

WHAT YOU'LL NEED
- a pen
- drinks
- several friends
- paper
- snacks

WHAT TO DO
Equip yourself and your friends with a pen and plenty of paper, a drink and, if allowed, some snacks. You've got a long and vital mission ahead. Imagine you are world leaders about to send a message about Earth to an intelligent alien race. You can send them 15 pictures, 10 sounds and five short pieces of video. What are they to be? Spend 15 minutes constructing a list with no peeking at each other's suggestions. Collect those pieces of paper and put them face down. Spend another 10 minutes refining your original list on a new piece of paper before discussing everyone's options for at least a quarter of an hour.

➤

Step 3: Going public?.............................

If the Men in Black not only exist but are in fact human agents rather than aliens, they would be working overtime monitoring all those people with vital information, and doing their best to make sure information was kept only to those who needed to know. Then again, the aliens may have made contact in such an incredibly public way that it would be impossible to keep it under wraps. If this was the case, it would simply be the biggest news story ever, eclipsing anything else that could imaginably happen.

How would people react? Some will be delighted and very excited. Many others will be very scared. The Earth's media would go into aliens overdrive. As many of the sci-fi movies and programmes around show hostile aliens zapping us poor humans, the authorities may have to release more information than they perhaps want to about the friendly real-life aliens to calm people down.

Money would be poured into building better space communications, to make contact faster and easier. Every single signal sent by the aliens would be exhaustively examined to make sure we understand what they are saying.

Step 4: In training, in position...............

Much of your training would depend on what Earth had learnt about the aliens or had been directly told by them. As the messenger from Earth, you would probably go through many crash courses in sign languages and other forms of non-verbal communication. What if the aliens communicated using telepathy? By the time you were about to make contact, there's a slim chance that researchers may have developed computer-based thought enhancers allowing us to receive and transmit basic thought patterns and signals. If that doesn't happen in time, expect to receive some severe instruction on how to shield your basic reactions and thoughts.

Where would the meeting be? That, and how the meeting could be conducted would be discussed for a long time. The aliens might be on a quite different scale to us, either much smaller or much, much larger, which could create difficulties. The aliens might not be comfortable with or capable of putting up with Earth's gravity, temperature or atmosphere. They may prefer to meet in space. So may Earth's decision-makers, partly to calm the nerves of Earth's population. There's a strong chance you would receive some serious astronaut training.

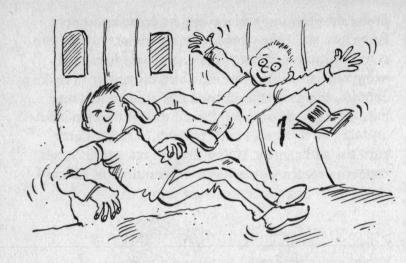

Step 5: Here we go! ....

This is it. You're about to stand face to face(s) with an alien from a distant star system. For as long as you can remember, you've had advisors and consultants buzzing around you telling you what to do and what not to do. But now, as the airlock opens and you're about to meet and greet officially for the first time, you suddenly feel very alone.

Those first few moments could be tense and nervy. To be honest, if the aliens were hostile or wanted you as a specimen to examine, you probably wouldn't know too much about it. You'd be zapped or tranquilized, stunned or marmalized in an instant. But, if they had made all this effort to make peaceful contact and were advanced enough to reach Earth from their home star system light years away, there's every chance they would not feel the need to kill and conquer.

Step 6: Question and answer time.........

You would run through the agreed methods of greeting and communicating, known as protocols. And there may be delays while mission controllers on both sides checked out the details. Finally, you and the aliens may start exchanging information and asking each other questions. Your first question would be out of your control. You would have memorized a list of carefully worded enquiries decided upon by committees.

However, you might get the chance to throw in your own. Choose it carefully …

The aliens would probably have just as many questions, and things to say, show you or communicate via thought waves as you. But to guard against mistakes, the first meeting would probably be kept short.

Step 7: What next? ....

The meeting over, you would return to base, be medically examined and have to go over what happened many times. Bet you wouldn't mind all the intrusions. You had done it – you had met up with aliens.

What would it all mean for life on Earth? Well if the aliens were friendly, it might lead to massive changes for the planet and its inhabitants. Over time, knowledge might be exchanged and shared, knowledge which could enable future generations to explore the galaxies, just like the visiting aliens.

Whatever happened after that first meeting, humans on Earth would know for certain that they're not alone. Our lives would never be the same again.